# A POET'S WHIM FOR SERENDIPITY

HRISHIKESH GOSWAMI

Made with ♥ on the Notion Press Platform
www.notionpress.com

## *Dedication*

*"This book of poetry is dedicated to all of the fantasists and believers, to those who never stop probing for the beauty in the world around them. It is for those who see the magic in the mundane and who find hope in the murkiest of moments."*

# Contents

# Contents

# Preface

Most commonly, poets use their poetry to convey their emotions. Still, these poets occasionally get the whim to do something occult. This book's central notion is pretty much like that. This book will lead you on a singular adventure that will undoubtedly alter the way you view the hitches in life and give your life a new flavour—something undiscovered. So, my acquaintance, are you equipped to go on this thrilling journey?!

These pages explore love and loss, hope and despair, as well as the intrinsic beauty and misery of the human experience. Every poem is a different window into my spirit, and as you read them, I hope you will identify with the feelings and perceptions I have tried to convey.

My earnest goal is that these poems, which I have poured my heart and soul into, may strike a chord with you and have a boosting influence on your life. I appreciate you taking the time to read my words, and I hope they may provide you some solace and significance.

With gratitude,
Hrishikesh Goswami

# Acknowledgements

Dear Readers,

As I turn the final leaf of this book, I am full with a sense of gratitude and humility. I am obliged for the opportunity to share my visions and notions with you, and humbled by the fact that you have chosen to expend your prized time reading my work.

I would like to extend my heartfelt thanks to my family, who have always been my chief supporters and have invigorated me to follow my passion. Their unwavering love and support have been a constant source of inspiration and I am truly thankful for their contributions to this project.

Finally, I would like to thank each and every one of you, the readers. Your support and interest in my work mean the world to me, and I hope that my words have resonated with you in some way.

Thank you for joining me on this journey.

Sincerely,

Hrishikesh Goswami

# Hrishikesh Goswami's Poetry Reviews

"...we were touched by the work and the communities reflected in your collaboration..."

-Su Cho

The Poetry Magazine

"Be very proud: your Poetry & Spoken Word submission, "Climate Change in a Humorous Attire," contributes to a growing collection of student work that is helping to raise awareness of critical ocean conservation issues, environmental justice, and the climate crisis. Young people like you are standing up, speaking out, and demanding action for their futures, and the world is listening!

We're excited to have you in this movement with us to create a safer, healthier, more resilient and equitable world for all."

-Linda Cabot

Founder and President

Bow Seat Ocean Awareness Programs

"We enjoyed reading your work and found much to admire. We wish you much success with your poetry." -The Editors

The Greensboro Review

"...we were impressed with your writing"

-Tanya Žilinskas

Invisible City

“Congratulations! We enjoyed reading "Nature" and would like to publish it in the July issue of Blue Lake Review.”

-Diana May-Waldman

Poetry Editor

BLUE LAKE REVIEW

“Dear Hrishikesh,

Your poems are beautiful as always. They are so deep and so mature. I could feel your vibes and pent up feelings!

Keep writing

Best wishes always.”

-Saikh Md. Sabah Al-Ahmed

Winner of the Reuel International Prize for Poetry (2019)

# 1. Existeth

*(Published by Guwahati Grand Poetry Festival)*

I know how grim it is…
It is to watch debauched things
Befalling in front of our
Very own
Very truthful eye
I have experienced the obscurity
Much enhanced today!
I have experienced the brutality
Much enriched today!
I have experienced the fraudulence
Much heightened today!
Just like a guiltless leaf
That has now crooked
Brown
Tolerating the horrendous Sun's passion
Rain's hassle
And winter's derision!
May this leaf '*Existeth*'.

# 2. The White Crease

*(Published by The Assam Tribune's Horizon)*

A keen white line
Ran confidently
Across the dark blue firmament
Quite clear
Quite sharp
Too smart to catch
To uninviting to explain
Too tough to apprehend
Is the meaning of this very crease.

*[Dear Hrishikesh Goswami,*

*Thank you for sending us your poems. We love "The White Crease" and would like to publish it in the next issue of Mantis. Thanks again.*

*Sincerely,*
*Gilad Shiram*
*Mantis]*

# 3. Rain Will Never Stop

No matter what you do
The rain will never stop
Never ever will it stop
Whatever you do will go
Nowhere but to otiose
Trees are crying
And sky is in pain
Birds are suffering
Animals are encaged
People are shouting
But in vain
The rain will never stop
No face
To be seen,
Of the mighty Sun
No noises of summer
No glow of colours
Only and only
Rain, thunder and lightening
All around the grey
Dull smelly cover
Poor children running
Mere kids spilling out of their schools
Looking wretchedly towards the sky
When will the rain stop?

Their plea which was earlier heard by someone
Are now only ringing like insect clinks of the backdrop
And finally
The rain did not stop!

# 4. Peace Seeking Mind

*(Published in 2022 August Issue of Cultural Reverence International Digital Journal)*

I can understand
The turmoil you have underwent
To hunt for peace
In the narrow constrictions of
The ruthlessly modern
Selfish self-seeking and malevolent world.
Where even to find a drop of decent hope
Seems grim or perhaps daunting.
In such a situation,
Talking about peace is inoperable,
Out of the box and most probably
Irrelevant!
For the quest for peace
Will show you uninviting faces,
And your futile hard work will
Feasibly harvest no good outcome
What you can do
Is to inculcate and create it within you…
And you will be
On the top of this scorching world!

# 5. Futile Meliorism

*(Published by Guwahati Grand Poetry Festival)*
*(Published by The Assam Tribune's Horizon)*
I thought the world was improving last night
But no! This morn
Everything was as normal as always but...
Suddenly
A bird flew over me…
Sprinkling on me
Few aerosols of hope and joy
Until I got to know
That this was only an illusion
A result of futile Meliorism!

# 6. Scrumptious Serendipity

How it feels
To touch the heaven,
To perceive its light,
To sense its presence,
And to discern your future?
I know it is a Scrumptious Serendipity
Something tough to explain and understand
For me and perhaps for you too!
But still let's look deeper into the voids
Appreciate their vitality in our lives
And hope for a Scrumptious Serendipity in them.
One of these days you may stand out
And say
Look at my work
I found a new way to look
Into things
And relish my life
Only because of Serendipity!

The PoeTree Contest

HOW IT FEELS TO TOUCH
THE HEAVEN, TO
PERCEIVE ITS LIGHT, TO
SENSE ITS PRESENCE,
AND TO DISCERN YOUR
FUTURE? I KNOW IT IS A
SCRUMPTIOUS
SERENDIPITY...

Hrishikesh Goswami

# 7. Preparedness

How prepared are you
Should be answered by your eyes
And not your mouth!
To tell me things
Or to listen to me
You have to be prepared
And if you are not
There might be failures
Or cessations in between our communication...
To ask me, "How prepared are you?"
You need to be prepared yourself,
For anything that is released
From your basket
Will return back to you one day
Even if you don't dearth that back!
This is nature's way
Of repaying loans
Which she took
From a bank
Which was not fully prepared!

# 8. Diplomacy

How smooth
And even does it looks
From the top
From the front
And from the back
But is it that artless?!
Diplomacy
Is an art
Quite simple and difficult
To understand
At once and for all
It is not what it is...
Diplomacy runs a body
And fuels a country
It guides you
Till you safely land
Or utterly crash
At or before
Your destination!

# 9. Politics

"Politics is dirty" they cry...
"We hate politics" some say
But why?
Is they any stable reason
Or the reason varies
From person to person
As well as place to place?
The answer resides in the question itself...
'Reason' is the answer,
As I feel
Politics won't be dirty
If there are apposite reasons
Behind every policy
Behind every action
Behind every planning
People seek for it
In the empty pockets
Of the 'Kings'
And when they don't find any
They start hating it
Calling it by various names!
Let politics run free
But under certain conditions
And reasons!

# 10. Bad Day

It is very laid-back to define
A good day
But to ascertain a bad day
From any ordinary
It's grim
At least for me...
A day is never bad
Until and unless
We edit it and try to decorate it
My day is squandered when
I don't find any visible change
In myself or in my work!
This perhaps holds for you too
But always remember one thing
The more you exploit a day
The more you earn out of it
And the more you earn
The more selfish you become!

# 11. Frostbite

It is strange
To have a frostbite
In summer!
But sometimes
I experience it
In my mind
In my conscience
Frostbite is treacherous
It prevents you
From exercising
Your full potential
And makes you impotent
To get out of it...
Melt it
With your toil, hard work
And stout determination!

# 12. Why Poems After Tragedy?

I have perceived a lot
Lot of people
Writing poems
After a tragedy!
But why?
The answer to this
Lies nowhere
Or everywhere
Poetry is pure reflection
Of the poet's mind,
It speaks for the poet
And helps readers
Understand the agony, despair and melancholy world within the poet.
Poet's are sensible to their surroundings
And so they can't avert their
Pen from scribing words of
Sadness, darkness and grief.
Let these poets write
On their tragedy
And let us read them
And appreciate
The poet's tolerance
Capability
And reticence

To diplomatically
Express his/her annoyance, contentment, lust, sorrow, grief and relief!
Let poetry be their medium
And let us not impede in this beautiful process
Of genuine poetry creation
At least for nature's sake!

# 13. Footwear

You have perhaps
Realise their significance
In our lives!
These foot wears
Embellish our feet
And guard them
From stuff like
Grime, sand and germs!
But don't you
Feel
The hostilities these foot wears
Experience while serving their masters!?
You may say they are inanimate
And there is no doubt in that
But what if these foot wears
Had feelings?!
What if they could speak?
What do you think will they say?
Nothing much...!
You are absolutely right
Foot wears have nothing to tell against us for they
Are created and destroyed
By us and without us
They will perhaps not be seen
Anywhere around!

*[“Very well written and expressive. I don’t think I’ll ever think of a pair of shoes as just ordinary again! Keep writing.”*
*- Diane Crawford]*
*[“Complexities of being stepped on are what inspired you with this rhyme. Thank you!”*
*-Kathleen Alice Mzoughi ]*

# 14. Mask

*(Published by Guwahati Grand Poetry Festival)*

How sweet
How mollified I was
When I met you
Gossiped with you
Abetted you out
In tough times
Perhaps only
In vain
For it was not you
Who was talking to me
Rather was your mask
Your veiled persona
Is soothing
Awfully nauseating
Go away as far as possible
Till your mask
Fails to cope up with your speed
Due to the vast difference
In the relative speed
And relative personality swings!

# 15. September's Glow

Who doesn't loves to relish
Evenings with September?!
I love September.
It fetches me an innovative ray of anticipation
Giving my static life
A new direction to move,
September is my rejuvenator
Uplifting my mind, physique and chi (spirit).
Its spark runs through my
Inquisitive veins
Permitting me to absorb more
Impart more and part more.
September's glow is justly appreciative
For it is distinctive and much more revitalising
Than any other radiance.

# 16. Neither

Do you know how hard it is
To say something
To someone who
Don't desire it?
Or do you know
How easy it is
To do something
That someone
Really want it to be done?
I suppose you know!
But I don't
Kindly tell me
Let me also enjoy
The happiness of knowing things
The feeling of sufficient;
The feeling of satiety!
Satiety is harmful I say,
You may not ask me 'why?'!
But I will still tell
For it is imperative
Satiety kills your longing
It kills your passion to hunt for...
Hunt for what...?
Money?!
Or happiness?!

Neither

# 17. Profit

We all know
That profit entices us
It pulls us towards itself
Much like a nail getting hauled
Towards the North Pole
Of any ordinary magnet.
But what actually is profit?
Does it mean loss to one party?
Does it mean?
If yes,
Then you may leave this poem here...
If no,
Then tell me why?
I know you will have plenty of answers
For you may want
Profit to rule this world
And you are not at all wrong!
Profit governs
And we get feeble
In Front of it!

# 18. Work vs No work

I love to work
Because it keeps me
Indulged and helps me
Identify new qualities in me
It unfolds new anticipations and ambitions
It helps me to design dreams for myself.
A dream is different from work
Here you labour but
Don't feel the genuine discomfort, worry or tiredness
The reason being…
Even I can't say
But yes,
A life without work is grim
At least for me
It makes me feel useless
It allows lethargy
To dominate my personality
It empowers evils
To cook in my kitchen
So dear,
Always discover work
For yourself
For it will
Keep you lively, renewed and '*young*'!

# 19. Arriving Winter

I am excited
To welcome winter
For I revel in its presence
It empowers me to
Love heat
To love the nature of warmth!
The beauty of the landscape
Outside the still window
Gives me gigantic glee
And the joy of living
The cheerfulness of youth
Winter is miraculous
A chest full of inspiration for
Poets and lovers
Who will ornament
The pages of the lonesome diary
Half occupied with summer stories!

# 20. Warm Food

The food you love the most
Is perhaps the one
That tastes a bit disparate to you
We eat to live
Or eat to relish
Food should be cherished
Warm food is distinctive
Palate quite matchless
Our physique is made out of
What we consume
And it keeps altering
Run-of-the-mill
For that is what
Is known as a
State of dynamic equilibrium.

# 21. Competition

Competition here,
Competition there.
Today world is crowded with range of competitions
Students brawl against each other
For a few seats or academic rewards
Competition builds up a spirit within us
To grow into the best
It is this emotion
Which generates a sense of fretfulness
Within us
And sows spores of hostility amidst us.
Tension and stress
Are words that mostly trail competition!
But life without competition is insignificant
As far as I feel
It makes us laid back and indolent
Quality of imagination will deteriorate
And nights will go dreamless...

# 22. When Time Stands Still

*(Published by Guwahati Grand Poetry Festival)*

Time matters more than Orlov for me,
Perchance for you too!
I always fantasise about
Time standing still
At least for nature's sake
But no…
Time doesn't want to
But if someday in the future it does
I shall be the cheeriest person
Of this self-interested planet
Of this abating humankind…

*["Ah, yes. Time standing still. All the time. Imagine how long you could take to admire nature's beauty without losing any time. This is how I see your piece of writing. Lovely job."*
*-Bella Russell]*

# 23. Hectic Life

*(Won honourable mention in the contest Quote Prompt - Paperweight. Poetry)*

Presently I am writing
This poem for you
My life is not yet hectic,
But who knows
What face the Sun might show up
Tomorrow
Life is a race as we are told
But for me it is something
Bigger than a mere contest
Something worth living
Something worth winning
You feel relaxed when you attain
Your anticipated goal
And perhaps halt for a moment
There is no detriment in it
But keep it short
Be ready for tomorrow's trial
Which might be
Very difficult for you to conquer
And thus stay humble!

*["A good reminder for us all, to celebrate our successes but to stay ready for tomorrow's trials."*
*- Paperweight.poetry]*

# 24. Casual Conversation

*(Published by Guwahati Grand Poetry Festival)*

I know you
Only because you want me to
Everyone wants to be known
And remembered by the person
One is speaking to
Even if they don't unveil it...
Our accomplishments will be hollow
If no one recognize them
Or for that matter
Recognize us...
So my friend
Live your life
The way that is not very tough
For the brain to remember…

# 25. Serene Outburst

*(Published by Guwahati Grand Poetry Festival)*
*(Published by The Assam Tribune's Horizon)*

The sky is as typical
Sun is on its way back home
The moon is ready to emanate
My heart is beating faster
Something unusual this sunset
Trees are tired of standing
And the wind is smoggy
The smell of pollution
No stars to view
No emotions to recall
The poet is wordless
Speechless and hopeless
Wants to burst out his…
But on whom?

# 26. Small Things

*(Published by Guwahati Grand Poetry Festival)*

What they do is
Recite gigantic anecdotes out of nil
Or in well-intentioned cases, out of 'Small Things'
They love to be silly, very silly!
They are injudicious and imprudent
This not only fits into them
But to most…
Small things will dictate our mind
Until we learn to worth
The primary things
That we do encounter
In the race of life.

# 27. Metamorphosis of Silent Dreams

Desolately only a few dreams
Turn into reality
But when they do
You get dumbfounded
Penetratingly stirred from within
Life is not mystic enough like those imaginings.
But fortunately dreams
Give shape to our choices
And our choices
Are solely accountable
For the metamorphosis
Which shall transpire
Just in front of your senses!

# 28. A Screenshot of Nature

The way the yellow leaves
With red adornment lay on the
Earth laden flooring
The way the tiny yellow florets
Ecstatically sleep on the
Punitive concrete
The way the vast spotless sky
Blends with the greenish brown meadow
The way the muddy waters of the
Motionless pond attract the
Monumental snakes
Defines my place
It is where I live
It is where I write
It is where I recite
A screenshot of this ordinary yet primaeval nature.

# 29. Workload vs Avocation

I would like to be a robust advocate
For avocation
But occasionally I feel
As if my backbone is craving for some
Hefty workload
I don't know why but it is
Maybe because someone is frustrating to
Expand the borders of avocation
To include a ludicrous amount of autonomy and morbid amount of pleasure.
Let them do what they feel like doing
But what about the others
Who are rambling in the path
Meant for that purpose
I feel pity for them
With that workload over their head
These souls will never have the opportunity to do
What their heart anticipated or what their minds told...
Why is life being unfair to them?
Tell me my cherished friend
For you too, have crossed your limits!

# 30. Poet's Sorrow: Yes or No

Sour
Bitter
But not sweet or salty
Is the taste of sorrow
It originates somewhere within
But is always felt at the heart
Why?
Why can't it be felt somewhere else...
Say for instance in the poet's life
In the poet's pen
Or in the poet's paper...?
The answer to this question
Lives within me
Maybe in you too
Nevertheless shut down your reason
And try to feel the heaviness of your chest when you are occupied with sorrow...
Now tell
Can such a hulking burden be handled by anything else apart from the chest?
No right?!
And so does it.

# 31. Selfishness: Inherited or Acquired

Those who are selfish
Are not born so;
They are engendered by society.
Society channelizes there trajectory
Towards a tapered chamber with
Neither doors nor windows
But only darkness
Pure pitch black
Tough to judge from outside
Is the condition of one inside
A poet can only feel
But can't help
For his hands are tangled
By the stern rules of the social order.

# 32. A Flower Of Hope

Everyday
No matter it is worthy or corrupt
Productive or valueless;
I at least find a flower of hope
But today
There is not a single
Who plucked away all my flowers of hope and happiness
He who did it
Is dancing now
Under the vibrant lights
Of pills, liquor and downers
He smells the flower
So hard that the flower has started to wilt.
Started to shed of its petals
One after the other
Till none of them is left to fall!

# 33. Now I Relish Solitude

Now I understood
The true beauty of solitude.
Far far away from those grinning faces
Which are not as straight as you might assume
Rather are cryptically coiled
Disparagingly aligned
And dishearteneddly displayed
In those portraits
Which are seen only once
Understood only once
But last forever
Last in the laxest corner of the poet's heart
Pinching and poking to find its way out of...
The poet won't let it go
Because they are the vibes
With which he is crafting a chain of thoughts intertwined
With well-dressed emotions
In the peaceful setup of solitary seclusion!!

# 34. When All Foes Become Cohorts

I envision a world with no foes
But only friends.
I will be able to roam in the alleys without fear
I will be able to sit and write
With flawless resolutions in mind,
And spot the smallest of the small
Around me with every ounce of my devotion.
No one to hate
No one to race with
No back biters
No leg pullers
Life will be as suave as margarine
And as untainted as fresh air
We will sit and stand together.
Eat and repose together
With no combat persisting
In the isolated bends of the realm and mind!
This is my envision about a world
With no enemies
But only friends...

# About The Poet

*(India Book of Records Holder for Poetry)*

*(Creative Endeavour of The Month April 2021 by The Assam Tribune)*

*(Recipient of India Prime Top 100 Author Award 2022)*

*(Recipient of India Star Icon Award 2022)*

*(Author of The Year 2021 Nominee)*

*(Recipient of The Leading Attainers Award 2022)*

HRISHIKESH GOSWAMI is a Contemporary Naturalistic poet from Assam, India who specialises in writing about nature and realism coalescing fiction and non -fiction in a sophisticated blend. Author of The Poet's Words, The Secret: Nature Reveals, Poems for Poets, The Exegesis, 72 Haiku, 51st Tanka, The Sesquipedalian Notion, An Aureate Opus of Quotes, An Ode To, The Arcane: The Adventures in Lavender, The Arcane: The Ultimate Fate, A Poet's Whim For Serendipity, A Fortuitous Odyssey, The Adventures of James Tony Morgan along with Co-Author of World Record Anthology Book – "Bilingual Aesthetics" and editor of the E-Poetry Anthology 'The Euphoric Verses from Soul' and the Literary Anthology 'Forest & Me' and 'The Idiosyncratic Mystery'.

Hrishikesh Goswami fell in love with writing from a fledgling age of 14 when he was at the 9th standard.

Hrishikesh Goswami's poems have been featured in The Assam Tribune, Blue Lake Review, Indian Poetry Review, the Weaver Magazine, Poets India, Soul Connection brought up by Guwahati Grand Poetry Festival, Anthology Still I Rise brought out by Wingless Dreamer, Winter Poems Anthology brought out by Poets Choice. Hrishikesh Goswami has been highlighted by Media Houses such as India Saga, Daily hunt, Spot Latest, Fox Story India, Glamwist etc. Hrishikesh Goswami is also available in E platforms like Story mirror, Anchor, Spotify, Wattpad, Google Podcast, Apple Podcast, Breaker, Pocket Cast, Radio Public, All Poetry, Listen Notes, Wynk Music, Poetry Soup, Commaful, Hello Poetry, SoundCloud, Poem Hunter, Scribd, Vivlio, Angus & Robertson Store, Mondadori Store, Thalia, Indigo Books & Music, Kobo Inc., Apple Books etc. for his dear readers. Readers can find further information about the poet in Google and YouTube by typing "POET HRISHIKESH GOSWAMI " for the same.

Hrishikesh Goswami has cracked several competitive exams such as JEE Mains 2022, NEET-UG 2022, CUET 2022, IISER IAT 2022, KVPY 2022,

AAU CET 2022, ASTU CEE 2022, IOQB-I and IOQC-I.

He has been bestowed with Certificate of Commendation in Never Such Innocence International Poetry Contest, Certificate of Achievement from Asian Council for English Proficiency Test conducted under CAFLR norms, Certificate of Merit for Outstanding Performance in NationWide Mega Science Experiment Conducted by NCERT, VVM, VIBHA and Ministry of Education, Govt. of India, Editor's Choice Award in International Essay Writing Competition by Monomousumi and is recognised by World Record University, Career Development College London, Guwahati Grand Poetry Festival, WWF India, APJ. Abdul Kalam International Foundation, ASSIST WORLD RECORDS, PONDICHERRY BOOK OF RECORDS and Royal Commonwealth Society.

He has been two times State Level Tae-kwon-do Champion, Gold Medallist of several National and International Competitive Exams and Olympiads, a KVPY Scholar, Winner of National School Level Essay Writing Contest conducted by Maulana Abul Kalam Azad Awards 2020, Grand Master of Mental Arithmetic-Senior A Whole Brain Development Program from Aloha (Abacus), Visharat in Hindustani Classical Music, Best Debater of PRARAMBH 2021 conducted by Nehru Group of Institutions, Kerala and Holder of Honourable Mention in several notable Poetry Competitions from around the World.

Apart from these Hrishikesh's poems have been critically analysed by Fruit Journal Manchester (UK), Acorn (A journal of contemporary haiku), The Leading Edge Magazine, BreakBread Magazine and has been published by The Assam Tribune's Horizon and Planet Young, NEZINE (An online magazine), Noverse Foundation and FoxGales Publishers, Poem hunter-The World's Poetry Archive, Cultural Reverence (An International Digital Journal Of Art and Literature), Tech Touch Talk of Kolkata.

Hrishikesh Goswami's poems have been read by The Liminal Review, Poetry London, Appalachian Review, The Tether's End, Tears in the Fence Literary Journal, MASKS Literary Magazine, Ribbons, The Hopper (An environmental literary magazine), The West Trade Review, Split Rock Review, The Baltimore Review, Rollick Magazine, The Poetry Magazine, Chestnut Review, The Sun Magazine, The Society of Classical Poets, The Greensboro Review, The London Magazine, The Kenyon Review, The Adroit Journal, Washington Square Review, Wilderness House Literary Review and many more.

Hrishikesh's haiku poem has been translated into Japanese and published in a traditional Japanese style literary anthology.

Nevertheless Hrishikesh's poems have been able to gratify the minds of critics to an extent and hopes to improve this range in the upcoming years. A few of his poems have also been widely accepted in Poetry Circles and Forums.

# Other Books From The Poet

*poethrishikesh.wordpress.com*

*&*

*poethrishikeshgoswamisbookshelf.wordpress.com*

9 798889 752745

Printed by Libri Plureos GmbH in Hamburg,
Germany